The
Connection Cleanse

Release connections to create more space for YOU with this 7 day guided cleanse

TRICIA SYBERSMA

HeartMath® is a registered trademark of Quantum Intech, Inc.
For all HeartMath® trademarks go to www.heart.com/trademarks

Print ISBN 979-8-9867969-7-0
Ebook ISBN 979-8-9867969-8-7

This publication is designed to provide accurate and authoritative information regarding the subject matter covered. It is sold with the understanding that the author is not engaged in rendering professional services. If legal, accounting, medical, psychological, or any other expert assistance is required, seek the services of a competent professional.

All imagery from Shutterstock.com
Design and layout by Rachel Rossano

The Connection Cleanse

Create space
for positive
and uplifting
connections to
flow freely

Which Experience are we in?

 GRATITUDE
*Experience Gratitude **for self** and
the world around you*

 CONNECTION
*Experience Connections **to self**,
community and beyond*

 ACTION
*Experience living **your life with awareness**
in the world around you*

Welcome to The 7-day Connection Cleanse

CLEANSE YOUR CONNECTIONS. CONNECT TO YOUR POWER.

The Connection Cleanse is designed to help you:

- Disconnect from external connections, distractions and emotions that may be negatively impacting your mental well-being
- Reconnect with specific and unique connections and emotions that strengthen you

Stemming from the book "The Connection Experience"

This cleanse provides a step-by-step guide to help you cleanse your body, mind and emotions from any unwanted connections that are causing stress, anxiety, or other depleting emotions.

The program guides you through a series of exercises and practices designed to help you to:

Identify and release any negative emotional connections

that may have formed with other people, places, or events.

Let's first look at the definition of emotion:

- a conscious mental reaction experienced as strong feelings and accompanied by physiological and behavioral changes in the body.

Emotions include fear and anger as well as joy and gratitude. What's important to note is, emotions influence our energy and physical body.

By disconnecting from these external emotions, you can experience a greater sense of peace, clarity, and emotional balance.

Whether you are looking to improve your mental health, reduce stress, or gain a better understanding of your emotional state, the Connection Cleanse Program offers personal transformation and growth.

DAY 1

What is Connection?

CONNECTION IS A STATE OF BEING IN WHICH
ONE FEELS A SENSE OF UNITY OR ONENESS
WITH ANOTHER PERSON, ENTITY, OR ASPECT
OF THE WORLD AROUND THEM.

What type of connections are there?

Connections influence all areas and aspects of our life.
These connections can be:

- Physical
- Emotional
- Social
- Spiritual; your relationship with energy

Physical connections

Can refer to the tangible and visible links between objects or people, such as wires or cables connecting electronic devices, or the bonds between atoms in a molecule.

Emotional connections

Are the intangible and often invisible bonds that we form with others, based on shared experiences, feelings, or values.

Social connections

Refer to the ties we have with people in our communities, such as family, friends, colleagues, or acquaintances.

Spiritual connections

Relates to our sense of interconnectedness with a higher power or universal energy.

In essence, connections are what make us human and give our lives meaning and purpose. They help us to feel a sense of belonging and to experience the world in a more profound way.

Mindful Questions

Learn how to become more aware of all the things connecting to you and to intentionally choose which connections to strengthen and which to let go.

Some questions to get started with:

- How do you understand your own connections?
- Do you see them as a physical connection, such as "I'm literally connected to my chair while I sit on it."
- As an emotional component, like "I'm connected to my child and when they are sad, I feel sad too?"
- Or spiritual, as in "I feel connected to my beloved pet who is no longer with me."

Ask Yourself

- How would you feel if you suddenly became aware of all the things actually connecting to you?
- Do you see yourself disconnecting from some things while strengthing your connection to others?

Disconnect from
what depletes you
and reconnect
to what
elevates you

Self-Exploration and Growth

Take some time to explore your inner self and identify areas where you'd like to grow. Allow yourself to be vulnerable and honest, without judgment or criticism. Trust that with self-exploration and intentional effort, you can create a fulfilling and meaningful life.

Self -Check

- Are you planning new goals for yourself?
- Organizing work?
- Making plans with friends and family?

How are these areas influencing your overall electromagnetic being?

What energy are you putting out, and what energy is magnetically coming back?

You can explore these answers by asking yourself how you feel.

Today's Intention

- Set the intention to become more aware of your surroundings and your own energy.
- Take notice of what's going on around you and how it's affecting you.
- Observe the emotions that arise within you during these moments.
- Recognize that your environment can have a direct impact on your energy levels.

Becoming aware is a huge part of the process!

*By cultivating positive and meaningful connections,
we can improve our mental, emotional, and physical
well-being, and enhance our overall quality of life.*

DAY 1

Special Notes

DAY 2

Practicing Conscious Awareness

INVOLVES DEVELOPING A DEEPER
UNDERSTANDING OF OURSELVES AND OUR
EXPERIENCES, AND CULTIVATING A SENSE OF
CLARITY AND PEACE IN OUR DAILY LIVES.

Practicing Conscious Awareness

Being Fully Present

Conscious awareness is about being fully present and mindful of the connections in your life.

It involves:

- Consciously identifying and assessing the quality of those connections.
- Disconnect from anything that no longer serves your highest good.

By being consciously aware of the connections in your life, you can take control of your energy and ensure that you are only attracting positive, uplifting connections that align with your intentions and goals.

This helps to raise your

overall vibration and

contributes to a more

positive collective

consciousness.

As you begin to identify the common instances that affect your state of being, whether emotionally, physically, or spiritually, you are...

on your way to connection awareness.

Mindful Questions

- When do you feel depleted? Notice what activites leave you feeling drained over the past few days or weeks, ie. *the news, work, family, something else.*

- When do you feel energized? Identify activities or habits in your daily routine that leave you feeling renewed and connected.

- What emotions or thoughts tend to arise when you are faced with a challenging situation or interaction?

Today's Intention

- To cultivate a deeper understanding of your self and how you feel in different moments.

- To become more attuned to your surroundings.

- To observe thoughts and emotions as you experience them, without judgment.

Through practicing conscious awareness, we become more than just passive observers of our lives; we become active participants in creating our reality.

Moments of Contemplation

Allow yourself the gift of contemplation by taking a few moments to consider these questions. Approach them with an open mind and heart, without any preconceived notions or expectations. Trust that within you resides the wisdom and guidance necessary to live a life that is authentic and satisfying.

Enhance

1. Rosemary Essential Oil

Incorporating essential oils into your conscious awareness practice can help enhance your experience. Consider using rosemary essential oil to invigorate your senses and promote focus as you delve into a deeper level of self-awareness.

To fully engage with the essential oils, try the following steps:

- Begin by dropping 1-3 drops of the oil into your hands and rubbing them together. This action helps to activate the energy of the oil.

- Cup your hands over your nose and take a few slow, deep breaths. This will allow you to inhale the aroma of the oil and begin to experience its therapeutic effects.

- Finally, you can apply the oil to your temples, being mindful not to get it anywhere near or in your eyes. This will help to further activate the healing properties of the oil and enhance your practice of conscious awareness.

*Take care to **only** use therapeutic-grade oils.*

2. Music

As you practice conscious awareness, consider incorporating healing music into your routine. With the help of "The Connection Cleanse Toolkit," you can access a variety of soothing sounds to help you stay grounded and focused.

Allow the music to guide you as you explore your thoughts and emotions, and let it support you on your journey toward greater connection and self-awareness.

Practicing conscious awareness of our connections allows us to see the world through a clearer lens, leading us towards deeper and more meaningful relationships with ourselves and others.

DAY 2

Special Notes

DAY 3
Field of Connections

THE WEB OF RELATIONSHIPS, NETWORKS,
AND INTERACTIONS MAKE UP OUR
EXTERNAL CONNECTIONS WITH THE
WORLD AROUND US. IT INCLUDES OUR
RELATIONSHIPS WITH PEOPLE, NATURE,
OBJECTS, AND TECHNOLOGY.

Field of Connections

The Field of Connections is a concept that describes the network of existing and potential physical and energetic connections available to us at any given moment.

This field includes our relationships with people, nature, our environment, and even with ourselves.

Having gained a new awareness about your connections in the previous sections, you can now choose to consciously engage with them in a positive way to enhance your well-being.

Like a web of light, the field

of connections weaves us

all together, reminding us of

the infinite possibilities for

love and growth.

CLEANSE A CONNECTION WITH YOURSELF

To begin, focus on cleansing one area of connection **with yourself.**

This means taking time to examine any negative self-talk, limiting beliefs, or self-sabotaging behavior that may be affecting your well-being.

It involves becoming aware of your thoughts and emotions, observing them non-judgmentally, and consciously choosing to shift them towards a more positive and empowering direction.

Mindful Questions

- Reflect on a limiting belief you may have about yourself.

- When did this belief begin?

- How does this belief show up and how does it make you feel?

- Do you want to continue to hold onto this belief?

Disconnect

- Recognize and acknowledge any depleting thoughts or emotions that arise from this connection you have with yourself.

- Can you consciously disconnect from this belief, even if it's just temporary?

- What would it actually feel like to no longer hold this belief?

- Take a few deep breaths and visualize releasing these thoughts or emotions from your body and mind.

Affirmations

- I release all connections that no longer serve my highest good.

- I am worthy of positive and healthy connections, and I let go of anything that does not align with this truth.

- I trust myself to know when to let go and disconnect from people and situations that drain my energy.

- My well-being is a priority, and I release any connection that jeopardizes it.

- I am in control of my connections and choose only those that bring positivity and joy into my life.

Reflections and realizations

Take a few moments to reflect on these questions, without judgment or expectation. Trust that your heart holds the wisdom and guidance you need to live a fulfilling and authentic life.

_____

_____

_____

_____

_____

_____

_____

_____

_____

_____

_____

_____

_____

_____

_____

_____

_____

_____

_____

_____

_____

_____

_____

_____

_____

Observation

- How does it feel when you declare to disconnect? Does it feel heavy, light, exciting, worrisome, or something else?

- Where do you feel it in your body? Do you notice any physical sensations such as tension, relaxation, or a release of energy?

- Can you give it a color? What color comes to mind, or did you see a color when disconnecting?

- Are there any thoughts or emotions that arise when you disconnect? If so, what are they?

Observing these sensations assists in the learning process. Making a clearer pathway to disconnect again and again as needed.

Enhance

Vetiver Essential Oil

You can begin the disconnecting process by getting grounded with vetiver essential oil.

- Add 1-3 drops of vetiver essential oil in your hands and rub them together to activate the oil's energy.

- Cup your hands over your nose and breathe slowly and deeply for a few seconds.

- Apply the oil to the soles of your feet and take note of how it feels.

*Take care to **only** use therapeutic-grade oils.*

The field of connections is a reflection of the energy we project and attract, shaping our external experiences and ultimately influencing our internal state of being.

EXERCISES TO

Support the Cleanse

BY CONSCIOUSLY CONNECTING YOUR
BREATH TO YOUR HEART, YOU BRING A
SENSE OF CALM AND GROUNDING TO YOUR
NERVOUS SYSTEM.

Scan to
watch

Heart-Breath Connection

Connecting with our inner selves can be done in many ways, but one powerful method is through the heart-breath connection.

By simply focusing on your heart area while breathing in and out with intention, you can experience rapid physiological changes in your body and open up the heart energy that is essential for self-connection.

To get started, follow the short video (QR code on pg. 28) that will guide you through a quick heart-breath connection exercise. Before you begin, take a moment to ground yourself, calm your mind, and become fully present in the moment.

Mindful Questions

- What does my heart want me to know right now?

- What values, passions, or dreams resonate with my heart?

- How can I show more compassion, kindness, or forgiveness to myself and others?

- What small step can I take today to honor and nourish my heart's needs and desires? Be gentle with the yourself, this is a process.

Enhance

Basil Essential Oil

Enhance your heart-breath connection with basil essential oil.

- Begin by dropping 1-2 drops of basil essential oil in your hands and rubbing them together to activate the energy.

- Cup your hands over your nose and breathe deeply, inhaling the aroma of the oil.

- Apply the oil to your heart area, gently massaging it into your skin or moving your hands in slow circles in the air over your heart.

- As you do this, focus on the intention of connecting with your heart and breathing deeply into this area.

DAY 3
Special Notes

DAY 4

Extending the Field

TODAY, WE WILL FOCUS ON ANOTHER AREA
OF CONNECTION TO BECOME AWARE OF AND
CLEANSE: **A PERSON.**

More cleansing in the field

Let's expand our understanding of the Field of Connection by focusing on one particular area today: our connections **with other people.**

Take a moment to reflect on the relationships in your life.

Is there someone with whom you feel disconnected, drained, or depleted? This could be a friend, family member, coworker, or someone else in your life.

Mindful Questions

- When did this connection start? How has it evolved over time?

- What are the qualities of this connection? Is it nourishing or depleting? Does it bring you joy or stress?

- How does it affect your daily life and well-being?

- What would it feel like to no longer be connected to this person?

Disconnect

- Can you disconnect from this, even if it's temporary? Take note of how it feels let go of this connection in this moment.

- Imagine what your life would be like without this connection. How would it feel? What opportunities could open up for you? Use this vision to motivate yourself to take action.

- If you find it challenging to disconnect, try setting a clear boundary instead. For example, you might limit your interactions with this person, or avoid certain topics of conversation. Notice how this boundary affects your energy and well-being.

Affirmations

- "I no longer choose this connection and disconnect with gratitude."

- "I release all negative energy associated with this connection, and invite positive, loving energy into its place."

Enhance

Binaural Beats

Enhance your connection practice by incorporating binaural beats. Put on your headphones and listen to "Binaural Beats for Connection" for at least 3 minutes or longer, allowing yourself to fully immerse in the experience.

Scan to watch

After listening, revisit the mindful questions to deepen your reflection.

Refer to the Connection Cleanse Toolkit for more music to support your Connection Cleanse

Sometimes, the most loving thing we can do is to disconnect from a person who drains our energy and dimishes our light, in order to **reconnect with ourselves** and shine brightly once again.

Reflections and realizations

Journaling can be a powerful tool in reflecting on your disconnection with a person and gaining clarity of your emotions and thoughts.

EXERCISES TO CONNECT

Heart to Brain

THIS SIMPLE YET EFFECTIVE TECHNIQUE
INVOLVES SLOWING DOWN YOUR
BREATH, FOCUSING ON YOUR HEART, AND
CREATING A COHERENT RHYTHM BETWEEN
YOUR HEART AND BRAIN.

Scan to
watch

Heart to Brain Connecting

Did you know that your heart has special neurons similar to those found in your brain? Connecting to these neurons is referred to as accessing your "heart intelligence."

What does that mean? Consider your heart as the gateway of emotional information to your body. Your heart is the commander, and it communicates the status of the outside world to your brain—the chemical command center.

If you are feeling fear, your heart communicates this to your brain, and the brain responds with a protocol that controls the rest of your body, including hormones, the nervous system, and all organs. It's pretty powerful stuff!

Consciously Connect

Let's consciously connect to these neurons and bring an uplifting feeling into our hearts and brains.

Follow the short video (QR code on pg. 36) while we breathe into a heart-brain connection.

Enhance

Rosemary Essential Oil

Bring in rosemary essential oil for heart connection enhancement

- Add 1 drop in your hands and rub them together to engage the energy.
- Cup your hands over your nose and breathe slowly and deeply for a few seconds.
- Apply the oil to your heart area, then at the top of your head.
- If you don't want to rub it directly on, just draw slow circles in the air over your heart area.

DAY 4

Special Notes

DAY 5

Continuing in the Field

FOCUSING ON CLEANSING A CONNECTION
TO: **AN EVENT OR PLACE.**

Cleanse connection to a place

Let's continue cleansing our connections by focusing on an event or place.
Is there a personal event or place that leaves you feeling low and drained?

Take a closer look and reflect on your connection to a specific world event, which is an external energy that can have a powerful influence.

- How connected are you to a personal event, place, and or a world event?
- How does it affect your day-to-day life?

If you feel a sense of heaviness or dread by the end of the day, then you may be more connected to it than you realize.

Mindful Questions

- Is the way I feel true to myself, or is it influenced by outside connections?

- Is this how I want to feel?

- What benefits might I gain from this connection?

- What disadvantages do I experience because of this connection?

- Do I want to stay connected to this?

Disconnect

- Can you visualize untying or detaching from the cord or link between yourself and the event or place?

- What would it look like if you released this connection? Try visualizing fall leaves in autum, or waves on a beach washing the connection away.

- How might you feel differently if you were no longer connected to this event or place? Can you imagine feeling more peaceful, content, and/or centered?

Affirmations

- I release all negative energy related to this event/place.

- I am not defined by this event/place, and I release it from my energy field.

- My energy is my own, and I choose to release all connections to this event/place.

- I am free from any emotional attachment to this event/place.

- I trust in my ability to disconnect from this event/place and move forward in positivity.

- I release all fear or anxiety associated with this event/place.

- My energy field is clear and free from any connection to this event/place.

Remember to be gentle with yourself and take your time with this process of disconnection. It may not happen all at once, but every small step counts towards greater clarity, balance, and well-being.

Enhance

Binaural Beats

After consciously disconnecting from a negative event or place, it can be helpful to continue the process by listening to binaural beats.

We recommend "Let Go of Negative Attachment," which can be played with headphones for at least three minutes, or longer if you prefer, to enhance your experience.

Scan to watch

You can also continue to ask yourself reflective questions during the exercise to further deepen your connection with yourself.

*Refer to the Connection Cleanse Toolkit for more music to support your Connection Cleanse

Reflections and realizations

Journaling can help you process your feelings and gain a deeper understanding of your relationship to it. So grab a pen and let's explore disconnecting from this external energy.

_____

_____

_____

_____

_____

_____

_____

_____

_____

_____

_____

_____

_____

_____

_____

_____

_____

_____

_____

_____

_____

_____

_____

_____

_____

EXERCISES TO CLEANSE

Lung Meridian

WE TRACE THIS MERIDIAN TO CLEAR
BLOCKAGES AND ENHANCE THE FLOW OF
EMOTIONAL ENERGY OUT OF THE BODY.

Scan to
watch

Lung Meridian Cleansing

Emotions can have a profound impact on our physical and mental well-being, and it's important to take steps to release any stagnant energy from our bodies.

Today, we will focus on tracing the lung meridian to help cleanse any emotional connections to an event or place that may be weighing us down.

The lung meridian is known to store emotions like sadness, grief, and heartache, so by working with its energy flow, we can help release these emotions from our bodies.

Consciously Connect

Let's focus on consciously connecting with our lung meridian to help release any stagnant emotions stored in our body. By tracing this meridian, we can promote the flow of energy and invite a sense of uplifting and renewal into our hearts and minds.

Watch this short video (QR code on page 44), to learn how to trace your lung meridian to help strengthen the energy flow and promote a sense of release.

Enhance

To enhance the energy and feeling, consider using essential oils such as eucalyptus or peppermint along with your crystal of choice. Take a few moments to ground yourself, and then join in this exercise to help release any emotional connections that may be holding you back.

DAY 5
Special Notes

DAY 6
Emotional Guidance

WHAT IS THE VIBRATIONAL LEVEL OF
YOUR EMOTIONS TODAY?

What is emotional vibration?

Our physical body is how we show up; it is how we know we are alive.
It is through your physical body that you experience everything.

Different emotions vibrate at different frequencies:

- Lower vibrational frequencies, such as those associated with fear and anger.

- Higher vibrational frequencies associated with gratitude, care, and compassion.

Our emotions are a valuable tool for gaining insights into our connections with others and our environment. Understanding the emotional frequencies associated with these connections can help us determine their impact on our well-being.

- Awareness of our emotions and their associated vibrational frequencies can provide insight into the quality of our connections.

- Lower vibrational frequencies, such as fear and anger, may indicate negative or depleting connections, while higher vibrational frequencies, such as gratitude and compassion, may indicate positive or fulfilling connections.

By using emotional guidance as a tool, we can actively work to cleanse and release negative or lower vibrational connections while strengthening positive ones.

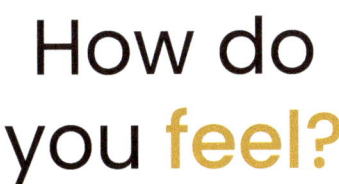

How do
you feel?

Track your Progress and Emotions.

Use this check-in to record how you feel each day and add any notes that you like.

By taking a few minutes to check in with yourself, you can build self-awareness, cultivate mindfulness, and stay motivated on your journey.

Whether you want to monitor your mood, track your habits, or reflect on your accomplishments, this daily check-in is your personal tool for growth and reflection.

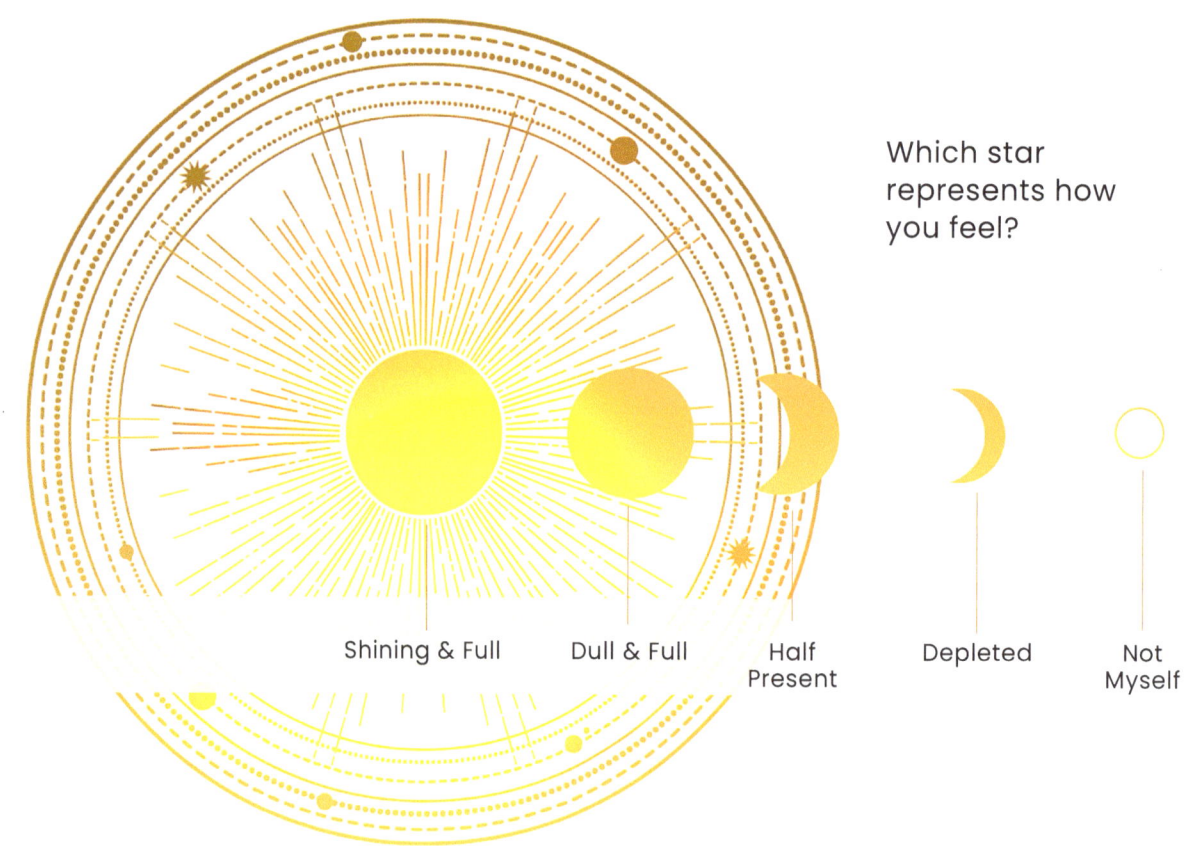

Which star represents how you feel?

Shining & Full   Dull & Full   Half Present   Depleted   Not Myself

Day 1 ~ rating and notes

_____

_____

_____

_____

_____

Day 2 ~ rating and notes

_____
_____
_____
_____

Day 3 ~ rating and notes

_____
_____
_____
_____

Day 4 ~ rating and notes

_____
_____
_____
_____

Day 5 ~ rating and notes

_____
_____
_____
_____

Day 6 ~ rating and notes

_____
_____
_____
_____

Day 7 ~ rating and notes

_____
_____
_____
_____

DAY 6

Special Notes

DAY 7

Navigating

NOW THAT YOU'VE LET GO OF WHAT
NO LONGER SERVES YOU, IT'S TIME TO
FOCUS ON WHAT YOU DO WANT IN
YOUR LIFE.

Navigating

You have worked diligently to disconnect from connections that you actively chose to no longer have in your field. Kudos to you!

This is where navigating comes in, a process of movement and attraction.
Now, let's choose what we DO want in your field!
This also ties in beautifully with manifesting.

The secret to navigating is to know WHAT you want to connect to and WHY.
This will help align your feelings to provide a clear path.

Choose a Connection

What connection would you like to bring into your field?
Think about what may bring you joy, fulfillment, and a sense of purpose.

The possibilities are endless, so choose something that resonates with you and feels authentic to your true desires.

Let's Connect!

- Can you consciously connect to this?

- Do you feel ready to connect to this?

- What color might the connection be?

- How will you feel when connected?

- What would it feel like to believe that you are solidly connected to this energy?

- Take note of any other senses.

Keep these pieces close to your awareness, especially the feeling of being connected.

This is part of the electromagnetic charge that draws connections to you.

DAY 7

Special Notes

Your intention, awareness, and beliefs form strong and active connections.

Integration

Journaling is a powerful tool for integrating new information and insights. Use this space to journal aha moments, and a plan for action to cleanse and optimize your connections.

Congratulations!

HEARTFELT GRATITUDE FOR JOINING US
IN CLEANSING YOUR CONNECTIONS.

Celebrate your Connection Cleanse!

Congratulations on completing the Connection Cleanse! Your commitment to cleansing your connections not only benefits yourself but also contributes to raising the collective consciousness of our planet.

Since connections are dynamic, you can use *The Connection Cleanse* as often as you like to keep your connections clean and free of clutter.

I would love to hear your thoughts on your experience with *The Connection Cleanse*, or if you would like to continue exploring this work, please feel free to contact us or consider adding *The Connection Experience* to your repitoire.

Thank you again for your participation in this important process. Until the next adventure, stay consciously connected!

With love and gratitude,

The Connection Collection

*Experience Connections **to self**, community and beyond*

The Connection Collection is a powerful set of programs designed to help you dive deep into the energy of connection for greater self-awareness and personal growth.

This collection provides a wealth of resources to help you stay focused and motivated on your journey toward greater connection and consciousness. Whether you're looking to break free from old patterns or cultivate a deeper sense of connection in your daily life, this collection has something for you.

The Connection Experience

You are invited to explore the power of connection for self-awareness and personal growth. Whether you're looking to improve your relationships, manifest your goals, or simply connect more deeply with your inner wisdom, *The Connection Experience* can help you tap into the power of connection and use it to create positive change in your life.

Your Connection Experience Notebook

A guided companion for *The Connection Experience*, providing space to record thoughts, quotes, and affirmations to support your journey towards greater self-awareness and connection.

The Connection Cleanse

A transformative experience designed to help you clear negative energy from your life and create space for positive, high-vibrational connections. Through a combination of self-reflection, guided exercises, and energy work, you can release what no longer serves you and open up to the possibilities of what could be.

The Connection Cleanse Toolkit

A powerful resource designed to help you cleanse and revitalize your energy. It contains a variety of tools and exercises that can help you disconnect from draining connections, and attract positive and uplifting energy into your life.

One Minute Manifest e-Mini

By taking just one minute to focus your energy and attention on your goals, you can start to attract the experiences you desire into your life. This practice aligns with the teachings of *The Connection Experience*, which emphasizes the power of connection and awareness in creating a fulfilling life.

Be Your Own Cheerleader e-Mini

Helps you tap into the power of self-belief and positivity to create affirmations that inspire and motivate you to achieve your goals. By infusing your affirmations with positive energy, you can cheer yourself on and accomplish anything you set your mind to.

About Tricia

Tricia was born in Toronto, Canada and resides in the Cayman Islands. Her passion for helping drives her to write, speak, and mentor others seeking joy, freedom, and unshakable personal power through Gratitude, Connection, and Action.

Being a HeartMath® Certified Trainer, a published author, and TEDx speaker, Tricia shares her inspiring and honest vulnerabilities to encourage her readers to be strong. She truly believes that navigating through valuable life lessons, brings new perspectives that invite readers to connect to their heart and live an authentic and fulfilling life. She has had many of her own opportunities to navigate life challenges with careers, parenthood, living abroad, adversities, as well as healing, and embracing life to the fullest.

"What truly matters, is how we experience our stories within the world around us. I invite you to step into the flow of Gratitude, Connection, Action to create a field of opportunity for positive change in your life."

Tricia Sybersma

The Gratitude Experience is a powerful and inspiring book that will transform your life by teaching you how to cultivate gratitude in a mindful way.

Learn how to shift your perspective and focus on the positive aspects of your life, even in the face of challenges and difficulties. By practicing gratitude, you'll open yourself up to new opportunities and experiences, and you'll start to see the world in a more positive light.

Start your journey of gratitude today and experience the transformative power of this life-changing practice.

Join the community to stay up to date on the newest books, e-minis, gifts and other offerings.

Email:

Tricia@TriciaSybersma.com

Website:

www.TriciaSybersma.com

Facebook:

/Ggnow2015

Instagram:

/triciasybersma

Twitter:

/tsybersma1

RedBubble:

/Tsybersma